In a Cabin,
in the Woods

THE GERMAN LIST

Michael Krüger

In a Cabin, in the Woods

Translated by
KAREN LEEDER

LONDON NEW YORK CALCUTTA

This publication was supported by
a grant from the Goethe-Institut, India.

Seagull Books, 2024

Originally published in German as *Im Wald, im Holzhaus*
© Suhrkamp Verlag AG Berlin 2021
All rights reserved by and controlled through Suhrkamp Verlag Berlin

First published in English by Seagull Books, 2024
English translation and notes © Karen Leeder, 2024

ISBN   978 1 80309 330 7

British Library Cataloguing-in-Publication Data
A catalogue record for this book is available from the British Library

Typeset and designed by Seagull Books, Calcutta, India
Printed and bound by Hyam Enterprises, Calcutta, India

Contents

In a Cabin, in the Woods

for Ariane

1

All this I see through my window:
a Sunday idyll under a blue sky,
kids in sheep's clothing feeding sugar to the horses,
something that used to be strictly forbidden.
Holidays at the pony park,
with death along for the ride, no saddle or bit.

I have to speak softly, so the flies
can hear me. They cast a light shadow,
that anxiously scutters across my window.
Now the first butterflies have started falling
from nowhere onto my attic window, birds follow suit.
The sun bleaches books on the windowsill.

Many of our greatest stupidities have proved
to be wise in the fullness of time,
a sage once said. But who was that?
My memory is a heap of broken bits
that resists any kind of order.
I pick a few of them out, hold them up,
to the light, at the window, and am amazed
at the richness, the lustre, the splendour.
But there is no connection, no continuation,
no 'image': the carelessness, which went into
constructing our world image that now begins

to crumble. I am stuck in quarantine,
my immune system has seen better days.
Every day brings new words to learn,
Today: herd immunity. Let's see how long
that lasts. No one says firmament any more either.
Enough of this naivety, unfathomable mourning!
I must patch up the fence before I die.
Where it's not held together by the ivy,
the reeds are broken. The crazy blue crocuses
on the meadow look like eczema.
With infinite effort I become a novice again
and praise the weeds, those useful idiots
that keep life in the garden ticking over.
That thing about stupidity—my grandmother said it,
Wittgenstein must have borrowed it from her,
you can't argue with that.

2

At the bottom of the steps that fall to the west
stands a body of water waiting for the midges,
that will plan their campaign here, later in the year,
when Helios is in the ascendant. Hades is still in charge,
but is preparing for the handover to Zeus,
who has already passed across this lawn,
so the ground-nesters know their place.
I must salvage the graveyard of snails,
their houses cast aside at the foot of the steps.
They died here without my ever having noticed,
and I always wanted to rehearse
the virtues of silence with them. Always
the four snail shells lying together,
like the four wheels of God's chariot:
Discrimination, Knowledge, Memory and Joy.
Gravestones that will not crumble in my lifetime.
Now is the time to read theology books,
to inspire a pneumatic enthusiasm.
For the road remains closed, the door locked,
the world must get by without people.
Fortuna and Fatum, non-identical twins, have the floor.

3

On the east side, just before the path to the Bismarck tower,
the trees have been felled, four mighty beeches,
all older and wiser and finer than the new neighbours,
who wanted a clear sightline, an uninterrupted view.
Given they've had to pay these ridiculous prices,
they want to be able to see their daughter riding
her pony to the tower, where the lads hang about,
who have no desire to inherit their parents' farms.
Bright rings of sawdust left behind as wreaths,
and the stumps protruding from the scratched-up ground
look like the crowns of three sunken kings.
The soil on the slope is dry and not very dark.
On the way to the tower, one would sometimes see a fox
in the dusk, stealing round the village like a thief.
But since the last five hens have vanished behind
barbed wire, the fox has gone back to the woods,
to catch an injured bird now and then.
The eagle on the Bismarck tower looks on unperturbed,
as the village changes. He, of course, knows
exactly what interests the lads. We haven't a clue.

4

Shortly before sunset, some time before six,
we permit ourselves a stroll, once round the block, so
I can replenish all I have stored away in my eyes,
or extend it, also to shake certain words
out of my head, mortality rates, for example,
words I now seem to utter without hesitation.
We stumble our way down to the lake,
without a thought as to coming back up,
which is torture for my lungs.
You must duck under the overhanging branches,
so the droplets of rain can do you no harm.
There is a certain smell that lingers here,
a residue of winter, I fancy. Watch out
for the roots, they're slippery, and you mustn't fall.
No one bothers to cut back the bushes any more,
they form a crypt from which you step out into the light
and see the lake spread suddenly before you.
You must wash your hands is all I can think of.
A bluish haze hovers over the lake, so delicate,
that then turns vivid red, as if daubed with rouge, and
from this frenzy of colour come the cries of birds,
great crested grebes and ducks. Cries of joy, I guess,
that we cannot see them, and they can't see us,
as we lean against the trees on the bank, caught between
a rock and a hard place, these trees that shelter our lives too,

bark dark with rain. None of these almost black trees
would wish to live in the city. And I would like to know
whether one can sense time as one senses a storm,
as one feels heat and water. How does one feel time?

5

Five metres wide, my window, four metres high,
the screen shot is always the same, in colour.
At five the green woodpeckers arrive and peck
their monotonous text into the soft ground.
They avoid the bare lime trees with their thatch
of twigs designed by Piranesi. Then the smaller birds
may take their breakfast, tits, blackbirds,
warblers and even smaller ones that, seen
from afar, look like butterflies. I see the wind,
when the grass suddenly gathers itself
to rediscover its shape, and when
the little birds hover trembling in the air,
watched by an inscrutable buzzard,
who waits on a post for his entrance.

But that is only half the story.
Because, naturally, in the afternoon I see
the forms return, the boundaries, the things
that can't be discerned if, at the same time
one's also reading up on how to live a blameless life.
One cannot understand one's own life.
How others should see me, that belongs in the past.
All the paths peter out, even the horses trot
wearily out of the picture, to the right, towards the Alps,

which should still be there, if what the scene
from the kitchen window shows is true.

I see how the meadow's getting greener every day,
I don't need that explaining by the man
responsible for the 'Inventory
of the National Mortality Register'.
Besides, anyone who watches the film twenty times
gets to meet the director. Gratis.

6

With the sun came the insects,
day labourers that vanish in the evening with the sun,
among them the idlers that sit on the tips of the grasses
letting themselves be cradled by the wind, that still blows
    from the east.
They don't hold a grudge if you flick them from their perch
with your finger. After all, one must learn to be good.
I am busy with the old stuff, papers dark with age,
because it's not right just to let them be, all those beginnings
of novels that were one day meant to change the world,
drafts of letters, crimson with shame, an essay on 'trust'
that I threw into the stove today, although paper does
    not belong
in the stove. All of them talk about this holy word, this God
above all the moral words that taste bitter in the mouth.
Be trusting and trustworthy, dear God!
In-between, I swallow my multicoloured pills, the names
remind me of Aztec gods, Venclyxto or Venetoclax,
and trust that they, like the bloodthirsty Aztecs,
who massacred everything in a conquered city,
will destroy all enemy viruses and germs. Once it was worth
cursing God when one had suffered injustice.
The midges are back too, though not the squirrels.
For three years they plundered my walnut trees,
now they keep a low profile in the hope

of getting a second chance. Forgiveness, another
holy word, Faith and Forgiveness, writ large or small,
these words should not be used for a while.
All the empty speeches will finish me off. But what I want
doesn't matter, living beings and things carry on,
keep evolving. I walk once round the house, the key
I tuck under the mat. Cars pass by on the horizon.
I'm being searched for but not found, not even the grass
knows if I'm still alive. This terrible willingness
to be everything, everywhere, was broken a long time ago.
But the squirrels could certainly come back,
so the magpies have something to squawk about.

7

Blood pressure is fine, though the rest could be better,
nobody knows where the noises come from, the crackle and creak
that steals into the heart first thing, the bubbling of fluids,
and when you walk past the mirror and spot the stony stare,
that's the best diagnosis. Even so, I go on upstairs,
to where my desk stands, under the eaves, already waiting.
Every day is a little greener, and the swallows are back,
and there's even a plane, because weapons are needed
in the sandy states that have to defend themselves
against proud have-nots with oil-smeared hands,
who all believe in a God who has forsaken them.
Since the trees have been felled, I have a clear view
to the plains of silence, the lands of discretion,
although the borders are closed and the shadow
has clung fast to the barn walls over the way.
One never knows what to think, the will to
speak the truth is no longer there, best to sit it out.
Why do you write all day long, asks a bird
that must have its nest nearby. It's the size of a tit,
has a face like a mask, a tight-fitting doublet,
and wings that look like stubby swords.
Daft question, I say, only idiots would hazard an answer,
let me look out on the landscape, white paper before me,
slowly curling up at the edges like a dried-out leaf
in the sun. The bird with the big, glistening eyes

and the self-satisfied pose sits on the window frame
like a classical actor, who knows the truth.
You belong to history, I call to the bird, and
you cannot touch history, as Robert taught us.
So scram! We're doomed to powerlessness, basta!
But I go into the open, lie down on the meadow, Hölderlin
in my pocket, and listen to the beetles, innocent itinerants,
who don't need pills on their bumpy road
into the beak of a bird.

8

Through the bare twigs I can see the glint of the lake.
In the sun it looks like a huge barrel of mercury,
about to spill over. The sky now is empty at last,
no planes allowed to fly, in the past one would have
said, God's hour is dawned. There's one exception,
the windowless, big-bellied, camouflage beasts,
that either fly over my head to inspect
whether I'm sitting at my desk, or are on their way
to poorer parts to offload their heavy weapons.
To ensure that a handful of Africans and Arabs can live
a successful life, in accordance with their own desires,
one needs, of course, lethal hardware. They behave
like children. But new birds have arrived that did
not introduce themselves. They stride the meadow
somehow forlornly, as though rehearsing for
    'The Word on Sunday'.
Close by, in Aubachtal, there are still lapwings,
the head waiters among the birds, but no one has time for them
any more. Yes, God's hour is dawned, no doubt about that.
All the flowers are so tiny this spring
that even the first bees fly past and ignore them.
Aquilegia vulgaris, the 'elf glove', as my grandmother
called the columbine, is scarcely there, the anemones
and violets, truly they creep on the earth. I can't
understand them but know what they say: you must

bow down to us, not look down on us,
like the liberal elites. So, I lie myself down on the earth,
small like Tom Thumb, lie down with buttercups
and harebells and wait without any impatience,
for God to either use His hour or indeed not.
In any case, that is to say, I am prepared.

9

I have set out the table in the garden,
between the two walnut trees, which are so dry
that the smaller twigs break off when the crazy coaltits
do their gymnastics on them. And suddenly,
the ants are also back, both the little red ones
that stagger across the tabletop as if drunk, in search
of the right way, as well as the larger black ones
that stand like proud nomads gazing into the distance,
before continuing their trek, unfazed by
whether the epoch of man is coming to an end.
As a child, I was always meant to read *A Struggle for Rome*.
But I preferred *The Soul of the White Ant* to the Goths.
And if I wanted to read about decline and fall,
it could only be *The Great White Gods* by Stucken.
When I look out over the meadow, over the peaceful
throng of yellow dandelions, I can't imagine
that something besides myself is falling apart.
The stars are still more precisely misleading
than all the political theories put together,
and the decadent desire to achieve immortality,
by shrinking into an information bundle
that can be kept alive artificially, seems
ridiculous compared with the labour of ants in their
subterranean realms, where things are rather more civilized
than on the surface. I see something that you don't, and it

will reach humanity as a normal message in a bottle.
But for that I need an ocean, humanity will not
be saved.

10

The cuckoo is back, the long-haul flier, still a little tired
from its nighttime journey over Spain, France, the Alps,
but I heard it this morning, after the news, as I stood
before the mirror asking myself whether it was still
    worth shaving;
as I greeted Cioran, Canetti and Blumenberg, all of whom
have asked this same question after the news, and the world
has nevertheless squeezed out another spring each year,
even if there's always something missing that cannot
    be replaced,
maybugs, for instance, that were only put in the world
to serve as supper for the cuckoo. Conservationists talk
of massive population losses when it comes to the cuckoo,
and the same goes for the field hare, the loner,
my friend, I won't even mention the nightingale.
Since she turned away from us or let herself be changed
into a barren switch, the relentless question as to whether
a shave still makes sense has become more urgent.
Best would be to veil the mirrors and only look in the evening,
after dar, in a windowpane or lake.
Hares can move their ears independently. The cuckoo
is back and looking for somewhere suitable to deposit its eggs,
it reckons with the idiocy or dubious tolerance
of other birds. Let it be as it used to be, before all the crises,
when the grey-mantled shrike and the nightjar

obligingly held their beaks when the nightingale began to sing
and the hare lifted its head above the furrows,
and the ducks did not suffer from histomoniasis, and I
could walk past a mirror in the morning without a question.
But it is not so, and never will be again.

11

Since the trees have at last begun sprouting again,
the wind has started giving garden concerts once more.
The St Matthew Passion is being rehearsed in the lime tree,
in the beech Bach's Chorales that bring you to tears.
And if you sit down beneath the weeping birch,
which itself looks like a precious tuning fork,
you can hear rarely performed works by Debussy.
The branches of the weeping birch touch the ground,
the east wind drags them gently across the grass,
so that beetles and other insects can easily
climb up like Jacob's ladder. I sometimes like
to wrap up warm and sit by the shed, in the spot
where two winds meet, as nature would have it,
and hear the water sloshing round my feet,
the sea on the doorstep, and Manfred Trojahn
next to me, explaining the secret languages of music.
Only the walnut trees are still bare, not a leaf in sight.
It's not a rebuke, their immune systems, like mine,
are up the spout. Even seagulls sail over the house
on the way to the fields on the other side of the road,
where they mess up the farmers' new seed.
And yesterday, when the wind dropped for a moment,
a flock of ducks flying above me towards the Alps.
You know how hard it is for ducks to lift out of
the water. Because they are so heavy, they have

to race over the surface like a plane on a runway,
that's what makes the beautiful, rhythmic sound,
and then off into the air, never to be seen again.
No idea what's going on with the walnut trees!
I know they breathe at night, xylem and phloem
seem to work, but why photosynthesis does not,
God only knows. They are supposed to be teaching
the squirrels. I pretend I know nothing about it.
In any case, music is not on the cards.

12

It's too dry. If you drill a hole into the ground
with your finger, you feel nothing but a trickle of sand.
No earthworm, no larva, no resistance.
No wonder the three-year-old apple tree, no taller than me,
a bit broad in the beam, hardly bears any flowers.
How lonely he looks in the meadow that shows off its
dandelions, like an old man, suddenly slipped from youth
to old age, with crutches under the thin branches.
Last year, its nights were graced with swarms of fireflies.
It looked like a luminous bundle of nerves,
and its days were plagued by butterflies,
with yellow vests that fell from nowhere
in surprise at our feet. The number
of dead is rising again. I caught two flies
with one hand and let them go. Do flies
feel fear? I followed a beetle with my eyes,
freshly varnished as if it had slept overnight
in an oil painting, moving through nature like Robinson.
Whither goest thou, quipped I. *Maybe this road
leads nowhere, but someone is coming from there.*
Stuart Friebert had sent me that this morning,
a poet from Oberlin in Ohio, friend of Günter Eich.
They are lines from a poem by Lars Norén,
translated into English by W. S. Merlin. All dead,
save for Stuart, of course. You must be in the wrong place,

at the wrong time, I tell the dandelions,
who celebrate their short lives like stone-cold virtuosos,
teeming with strength, despite all the drought.
What is left when I have prayed away the long catalogue
of bitternesses? I don't want to take part
in the ritual counting of the dead, yet I notice
how my hands twitch. Back to the grass, to the beetle,
to my poor little apple tree. I have to give things
a truth they cannot find by themselves,
otherwise everything dies on the vine. Me too.

13

There must be a crack in the fabric of the house,
the candle flickers as if it can't decide,
and the piece of paper on which I'd been
scribbling all day long, trying to find a beginning,
lies on the floor, butter-side down.
But the doors and windows are all tightly closed.
A beginning of what?
The day began with me needing to catch my breath,
going out for a spot of fresh air and meeting a friend
by the front door, whom I hadn't seen for forty years.
He'd seen better days, a broken wing dragged
on the ground like a cape, but I recognized him straight away:
a maybug. He didn't look like a baker, an emperor
wouldn't have visited me, so it was a chimney sweep.
A wind must have risen. Somewhere near here
lives death but he goes incognito. Everyone is impressed
by his cunning as he enters the houses unseen.
Later I sat down at the table and searched for words,
others have too many of them; I have none.
The Menachot says: 'There is a man who is destined
to be born after many generations, Akiva ben Joseph
is his name; he is destined to derive from each
and every thorn of these crowns mounds upon mounds
of laws.' I desperately search for words.
To ease the pain of my shingles, I have used

apricot kernels for exorcistic purposes, and a plaster
with active ingredients. Before my window
the blackbirds go around like priests, visiting a pestilent
village. I don't see what is happening in the world any more,
I have to read up about it. A world in collapse, many say,
but in my window I see only the beautiful sides,
regardless of what is written on paper.
In the evening I lit a candle because darkness
fell and threatened to suffocate me.
But the candle flickered so much I put it out.
From each thorn of darkness mounds upon mounds of laws.
Tomorrow I'll make a start.

14

Today I get to read Thursday's newspaper, so
it must be Sunday. The air is so limpid and clear,
that here, from my desk, I can see the flies
stuck to the shed. In the real world, if it
exists at all, they believe in artificial humans,
that will finally advance the abdication of power
of the real ones. Oh, to have a copy of our world,
but cleansed of all life. A well-oiled robot
should then determine our life: one fed with
every branch of philosophy that all find
their rest in him.
Our life. When I was in the village this afternoon,
the garbage bags were out on all the garden fences.
From the garbage one might deduce the social logic of
singularization, there's enough material anyway; on Monday
it's collected. Does anyone recall Professor Mandelbrot?
Him and his apple dolls. He was awarded an
honorary doctorate by Johns Hopkins, where today
they count the dead, and saw fractal structures everywhere,
also in music and stock-market prices. Things don't work
quite as smoothly as one might think, he said,
who was born in Warsaw, fled from the Nazis,
and died in Cambridge, Massachusetts,
each thing has a rough surface that you can't see.
Clouds like crumpled paper. No one on the road.

Behind a window I saw a child who jumped,
when it saw me, it looked like a sleepwalker
who suddenly awakes at the edge of the abyss.
Sustainable, the word on the bulging garbage bags,
but, I've learned, only the gods are sustainable.

15

It's raining. Insects gather under the porch roof,
and occasionally a bird dives in amongst them.
They are newly arrived, noble creatures with blue-grey jackets
over a bright vest. 'Nuthatches', Ute said yesterday,
they can creep down the wall head-first and feed as they go.
Birds have been around for about sixty million years, and
for just as long there have been insects that are eaten by them,
one of those weird business models created by evolution.
At some point in the midst of this state of permanent stress,
when no one expected it and teeth had got smaller and smaller,
we arrived and with us the choice between solitude
and community in paradise, which was thought to be square.
White Caucasians, one of those faded motifs,
which suddenly appear on the bull-necks of hooligans
and on the leather jackets of the Hells Angels Association.
Nuthatches, upside down on the outer wall of the wooden house,
where hopefully they will catch the horseflies from next door,
whose horse-blood has gone to their heads. The first man
came from the world of the North Star, the Gospel of Salvation
from the East, the Great Builder from the South, the God of Life
from the world of the West; and all of them surveyed
the brand-new construction, the new square paradise.
The pandemic is lurking in every corner. I won't be around
to discover whether we will all disappear or whether
the statistics are fake, but one picture will stay with me

to the end of my days, the cemetery for the poor
in New York, on a rotten island, with pine coffins
stacked on top of each other and hastily buried,
because it must happen quickly with death.
In the evening it brightened over the lake, the sun,
already almost drowned, became visible for a long moment,
so that I, immersed in the histories of epidemics,
suddenly didn't know if I was watching a sun rise
or its setting. In any case, I realized,
that I have learned the wrong thing all my life.
Birds that can climb head-first down a tree trunk:
this is more than the wisdom of fools.

16

The storm has passed, though every now and then
a rumble of thunder is heard, a timid growl,
as if Shango, the thunder god of the Yoruba,
was collecting his kit and hiding it in the Alps.
In fact, Hölderlin was the poet of thunder,
now Corona has deprived him and us of celebrating
of his anniversary. 'Though distant is, at springtime,
the lament', Scardanelli wrote into his notebook
on 3 March 1648, and we will stick with that.
Thomas, my poetic Chinese friend, writes that he is reading
'Bread and Wine' on the balcony 'no one bore
life alone; shared, such fortune becomes a joy;
exchanged with strangers, it is jubilant, sleeping,
the word's power grows.' I have to read the poem
straightaway, 'For a long time, and in the distance,
thunder sounded', before a new storm veils
the vista once more. 'This is the summit of thoughts
and joys, this is the holy mountain height, the place
of eternal peace, where noon loses its sultriness and
the thunder its voice.' I've made a fire,
before the wood in the barn gets too damp to burn.
Behind the logs, the blackbird has built a nest
and scolds me for disturbing it.
One of Shango's wives cut off her ear
and mixed it into the god's food, to please him,

but nothing came to fruition. '. . . no one bore life
alone!' I know, alas, too well what that means,
though distant is, at springtime, the lament.

17

Grey sky, we can hear the sea when we open our ears.
The grass in the meadow opposite is now so high that two horses
are not enough. Sometimes the head of a blackbird emerges
from the foaming green waves, like the heads of seals in
    Martha's Vineyard.
Where there are young seals, the shark is not far away, said Ronnie,
our host, who could read Plato on his computer and did.
Later, Ward Just came by, the best reporter of the Vietnam War,
for the *Washington Post*. We sat on the terrace of Ronnie's house,
drank gin and tonic and watched the otter in the pond,
who had known Thoreau and Emerson personally, *Walden, or
Life in the Woods* was his favourite book. Thoreau's cabin
looked something like the wooden house I'm writing in now.
Every year on the 4th July we sat on Ronnie's and Reni's terrace
reading and celebrated the United States Declaration of
    Independence.
Every day I look at the Bismarck monument in memory
of the German unification of 1871: forever the same picture
that is never the same. On top of the Bismarck monument
    is an eagle
with open metal wings, in cloudy weather it likes to take a turn
but is back on time when the weather clears.
The crows tried in vain to oust him from his pedestal.
Just in time for the 4th July, Bob Silvers also came over
    from New York,
he had four thousand books in his head and the first copy

of his magazine, which no one had read yet but us.
It's a good job they did not live to see the 45th president,
who, by the way, is three years younger than me. Around me
there are also heaps of books, life itself has sent them
      into the house
in opaque boxes. The murky masses of the conceivable,
trimmed to a handy format. Work, says Thoreau, should
      be more
than just securing a livelihood. That is why Herr Diess (VW)
wants some extra taxes on top of his bonus. Now everything is
on a drip feed, you can really let rip. No beautiful country
in this time. When I greeted the lime tree this morning,
it whispered to me (yes, really, it whispered): if you only knew
      my roots,
you would value me in a completely different way. But then
      I'd be
dead! Give me time! Now brothers, good night, the Lord
in high heaven has us in his sight, in his goodness, he deigns
      to protects us.

18

On my way to the post box today, so as keep in touch
with the tax man, at least, a cat came towards me.
We didn't know one another. She paused, her left paw raised,
leaning against air, as Zbigniew Herbert observed of a statue
     of Nike.
A gust of wind puffed up the hairs on the back of her neck,
it looked like a halo, illuminated from behind.
She has already had several of her lives, went through my mind,
Maybe she can help me? The church opposite the post box
is dedicated to Saint Valentine, the patron saint of beekeepers.
He was beheaded, for a long time the normal method
of dispatching a troublemaker. I saw relics of the saint
in the cathedral of Wrocław when I visited Tadeusz Różewicz,
the Polish poet. There are also relics in Santa Maria in Cosmedin
in Rome, even in St Stephen's Cathedral in Vienna and a hundred
other churches. The cat can take care of bringing them together.
Valentine was invoked in case of insanity, epilepsy and plague, so we
have need of him. In my church here, a crippled girl is said
to have crawled round the altar three times and been healed.
The church stands on a grassy pedestal overgrown with
dead-nettles, they look like dwarf cardinals, the colours
of their robes as fresh as those on the frescoes in Pompeii.
The plague in the Middle Ages lasted eight years, then it was done,
and a white piece of linen was pulled over the stained shroud.
Valentine was tired of always being asked to assist with illnesses,

so he also took on love, of which he understood nothing.
The plague, by the way, was brought from Central Asia via
    the Silk Road
to Europe. Allegedly. These days no one has got as fat
as the conspiracy theorists with their swollen hearts,
who sit on the bench in front of St Valentine's and offer
    cheap medicines,
as worthless mirrors and talismans were offered in the past,
to drive away evil spirits, bronchitis and anthrax,
in other words, everything that belongs to an authentic life.

19

It had rained again. And when it was clear
who would win the fight, I set myself
in motion and ran across the main road
into the forest, towards Münsing, to breathe in
the scent of nettles in the late sun.
If someone were to ask me about my childhood,
I would point silently to warm stinging nettles.
I walk over the footbridge into the wet, acid bog,
where fat selfish blueberries don't keep their distance
from the lily-of-the-valley, 'its pale heads heavy
as metal', as Moritz Brandt translated it,
one of the very best readers of Ted Hughes.
Hughes had an aggressive relationship with death,
before and after the demise of his wife Sylvia Plath.
Sun-hot stinging nettles, like warm bread and
overripe blackberries, to stick with the B-words.
That these blueberries will not bear fruit later this year
is because of the moor, which they call 'Moos' here,
or bog. If you walk along the Lüssbach in the evening,
the dead rise from the ground, like convicts,
in pelts of dirt, they stand bodily before you,
bathed in a sickly glowing light.
In the wood stands a house, the windows all open,
so that the souls of the dead could rise up,
that one day should be called the salt of the earth.

But if the salt has lost its flavour, with what will it be salted?
says Matthew, it is then good for nothing, but to be cast out
and trodden under the feet of men.
The idle wind has dug its claws into the yew trees,
whose branches are bobbing as if they were out to
give blessings, perhaps too much of a good thing,
but still better than no blessing at all.
'The message of the yew tree is blackness—blackness
and silence', as Sylvia Plath claimed.
Next to the house, under the leaky gutter,
stands a barrel filled with rainwater. A single drop
would suffice. But I must go back to my house,
to recover the unfortunate words,
before the raging Lüssbach bursts its banks.

20

In praise of rain! These last few days, it has seen
everyone off, so I could take one of these long walks
over the fields unhindered, without caution or mask.
There was not yet much to see of the corn
that is grown here, but the barley had bolted, and because
the sun on the other side of the lake, near Bernried,
had staged its bloodbath before sunset,
a fine red glow lingered on the awns,
and when a peaceful wind drove into the barley
and literally turned their grainy heads,
I suddenly had the Red Sea before my eyes. Right there
'on the site of the fabled paradise', grain was
first cultivated, according to Friedrich Körnicke,
in his *Handbook of Grain Cultivation* of 1855,
and many generations of sheep have spread awns
in their wool throughout the Christian world,
I love sheep and would like to be one of them.
I can remember my awns well, during harvest
they stuck to my back in my sweat and could
scarcely be ousted by dousing them with water.
This task belonged to one of the girls who came
in the afternoon to load sheaves onto the wagon with forks.
I passed Aufkirchen and continued through the fields
in the direction of Farchach, the awns on my back,
and thought in despair of Greek and Roman botany,

thought of pulse and spelt and the old bread-wheat,
to prevent myself thinking about the previous day's TV shows
that take over my brain with their rubbery honey.
From the pointed mouth of the burgher flies the nasty phrase:
Enough is enough! The time has come! We must finally act!
In Farchach there are two pigs that I knew from before,
when I was still allowed to enter the farm shop unmasked,
and goats that bleat quietly when the oats prick them.
It is not tiredness that forces me to take a break,
but perplexity: thank God the world is coming to an end,
then we will no longer have to endure the blather.

21

I should be blessed; every day I follow the flight of birds
and shun transgression, as Hesiod saw it, the master
from Ascra in Boeotia, who tilled his own field.
I also live in the countryside, albeit an enforced existence,
and if the illnesses run their course before the end of my life,
I can go back to the city to the crows and blackbirds,
that guard my three apple trees in the meantime.
Those who live outside the city walls are either wild animals
or gods who no longer thirst for recognition.
Athens or Ascra: the question no longer arises since the country
has become a part of the city; likewise Athens or Jerusalem
is not a puzzle any longer, since people only speak of Brussels
or Berlin, where you can now grow carrots on flat roofs
in order to be well prepared for the next crisis.
Today is the 15th of May. On 15th May 1933, Comrade Stalin,
the little father, whose heart beat loudly for the arts,
sent the poet Ossip Mandelstam to a labour camp
that he would not leave alive. Was it Hesiod,
who recommended making a list of all that should
be hidden from Zeus? In a clever book, I found this phrase
from Whitehead: 'Knowledge doesn't keep any better than fish.'
Of course, I don't know whether this is just a pleasing invention,
because I found it in the work of a philosopher
who could no longer have known Whitehead personally.
But these philosophical questions have plenty of time, I

by contrast, may not allow the opportune moment to pass,
to be happy, and if all else fails, I will swallow down
Novalis three times a day, an analgesic,
that must be enough to endure house arrest, for starters.
But what, for heaven's sake, lasts longer than three days?

22

I don't see any people any more, in these parts,
but occasionally hear laughter from behind a hedge,
where the path goes down to the lake. And, of course,
I know that people still bring the post,
which they deposit behind the hazelnut bushes.
Then again, two huge hornets came to visit today,
noble creatures that carefully inspected the books
lying about and immediately landed on the Hesiod,
lying open on top of the *Collected Poems*
of Zbigniew Herbert and on *Un altro sogno*
by Lina Fritschi, the blind poet from Piedmont:
Mi congedo dai versi. Forse dalla vita. Addio, addio . . .
The hornets likely live in the walnut tree,
behind the broken bark, in the brittle dead wood.
Unfortunately, I don't have Pliny's *Historia Naturalis*
with me, the 11th book dedicated to bees, wasps
and hornets—whose reputation precedes them.
While the bees and the white goat Amalthea
cared for little Zeus with honey and milk,
hornets bit the heads off flies,
and devoured their bodies, as the law bade them do.
A hornet has landed on my writing pad,
highly strung, as if its nerves and hot blood
and its sting were not at the end of its divided body,
but on its head or in the mouth like the common horsefly

that the horses next door send over to my house in swarms.
Politely, I escort the hornet to the open window,
where the crickets can now be heard. There is a well-known case
of a woman from Vilnius who had an unfortunate fall on the ice,
whereupon a swarm of crickets emerged from the wound
and died in the cold. This is not a case of bugonia,
in which whole bee colonies rise from the still-fresh intestines
of dead cattle, as reported in the *Georgica*.
How long do hornets live? On the sheet of my pad
I scrawl: this page was written by a hornet.

23

Five o'clock and there's the cuckoo. If it's actually true
that each call stands for a year of life, I would have to
stay alive for another hundred years, sadly without money,
because I didn't have a chequebook about me at that hour,
and probably without hedge sparrows, which will have
left for foreign parts by then. Hoffmann von Fallersleben
made the pesky two-syllable bird immortal.
Your refrain was not in vain, but a donkey might say the same,
and if Beethoven had taken pity, it's the donkey we would hear
on the radio every day this year. That scene by the stream
in the symphony isn't right, says the two-syllable donkey.
Later, I tell the story of my old age to the friendly doctor
at the clinic who monitors my blood count.
But he doesn't sing your refrain was not in vain,
and instead attaches me to the gibbet with the drip.
I'm standing on the top floor by the window, on the horizon
I see the Alps, above them a duplicate of soft material.
If I set off now, it would take me three days,
right at Garmisch then on up, if my heart was in it
and my infusion-God, Obinutuzumab, dripped more slowly
than now. Could you take a picture of us please, I am asked
by a woman whose husband is also on a drip, one belonging,
though, to another god. Give us a laugh, I call to the man,
who, despite his mask, looks as if he has never
laughed in life. I take three pictures, one of them

will be the last. The woman smiling on all three, if
I'm not mistaken. Lynghi, by the by, counted the cuckoo poem
among the half-dozen by Fallersleben that will survive.
When I get home, I will immerse myself in Rühmkorf's work,
pick out my twenty favourite pieces and listen to Mahler,
to the Humoresques from *Des Knaben Wunderhorn*,
Cuckoo vs Nightingale, Magdalena Kožená and
    Christian Gerhaher
singing the praises of the high mind, with Boulez conducting.
I have a hundred years, after all, and all I have to do is fight.
War, it says in Hobbes' *Leviathan*, does not only consist
of battle and the act of fighting, but also in the time,
wherein there is the known disposition thereto.

24

The wind has done its work: the sky is swept clean,
wordless and speechless, purged of any hint of a narrative.
As I sit here, I begin watching the impudent jay,
hopping through the grass like an unlawful intruder,
but cautiously, as if he were playing pickupsticks, yet
    clumsily too,
for the grass collapses behind him and only springs up again
when the air is clean and a future seems possible,
as if a delicate clockwork mechanism were hidden
    underground.
While I sit almost motionless under the walnut tree,
consuming hardly any energy, everywhere on the planet
people are working like crazy to save humanity through
the speedy annihilation of the world. It probably has to
    be that way.
Or do you know another way out? There is no BACK button,
no going back to nature. So, you perch the molecular glasses
on your nose and read the billions of letters of the genome
in a single blade of grass, in eight blades there are
as many letters as in all the books ever written.
And if something doesn't suit you, just take the gene scissors.
I am one of those who came into the world old.
For me, nature should always be beautiful and terrible,
and a jay in the grass is a turning point in world history,

if that's how you want it. *Dreams are good*, John mails me, *for me at least, because they are proof of sleep.* I'm on good terms
     with grass.
Maybe I'll manage to describe a single blade once more,
after all. 'When a gentian succeeds in raising its head
and flowers, the whole deep spring sky is captured
within', writes the 'Karst' poet, Scipio Slataper.
Here, suddenly, a love-lies-bleeding blooms, and I wonder,
who turned a switch on which network so that it flowered here,
and who gave it this terrible name.
When I have time, I'll dig it up and plant it on a traffic island
in the city where it can realize its full potential,
looked at by thinkers with no fixed abode,
and their passengers.

25

The coffee machine has given up the ghost, a Lavazza
from the last century, a linguistically gifted gadget
that could gurgle, groan, moan, hiss and beep, a miracle
of sounds all emitted in the course of producing an espresso.
But what an espresso! If the kitchen is still icy in the morning,
I hug my cold hands around his heating body
and talk to it while I watch the birds from the kitchen
window that are already having fun even now.
Two blackbirds peck at a patch of lichen that has formed
on a boulder, as if possessed. They look like disciples
of Michelangelo. If they carry on like this, maybe they will
have carved a figure out of the stone in so many years.
The aroma of a single Lavazza espresso changes the smell
of the whole house. Even the elms talk to each other,
I have known this since childhood, today a forester
is making a massive fuss. Even now my elms are perfectly
    translating
the light-harvesting complex into chlorophyll, a rich, light green.
That will remain or return when the time comes.
Only the espresso machine is done for, there's no more coffee.
Even human beings as a species will have their self-imposed end,
as one philosopher confidently asserts. Is it still possible?
One will survive, and he will come to me out of the future
along the lake and tell me everything; I will have known nothing
of any of it. And perfection is without complaint.

26

for Karl Heinz Bohrer

I was advised to get in touch with angels
or with the ancient Chinese. The issue itself is simple:
my lazy spleen produces too few white blood cells.
Long brooding has damaged it, the many worries,
sitting for long periods at a time with poor posture, nutrition
(tomatoes for breakfast, with coffee if possible!).
My whole life was a life lived against the spleen,
against the mother of all other bodily organs
and the source of all life energy, qi.
Now it's time to put the water glass on a yellow background,
take honey, marjoram and celery seeds, mix them well,
add sticklewort and hart's-tongue fern,
also ground ivy and young nettles, if to hand.
And then nothing better than out of the rat race
and on the way to freedom. Something must be done,
to boost the spleen in its efforts to break down the abnormal
blood cells, the excess of ageing blood corpuscles,
all the garbage that is temporarily stored in the spleen,
to make room for monocytes and lymphocytes,
for the good things that could lead to a good life.
Let others be burdened with care, stand in the way
of suffering, give coins to the beggar,
without embarrassment, and the rest to the state.
The clouds today look like huge cream puffs,

no one wants, they are forbidden; like soft cheese,
cow's milk, sugar, yogurt and red tomatoes,
and, of course, no mention of alcohol and tobacco,
because we want to dedicate ourselves to good digestion,
for only it, along with a pure spleen, are the guarantors
of a proper life after a premature death.

27

At some point you realize that you are there
to say goodbye with helpless words.
The crack of dawn was long ago,
the pale glow on the underside of the poplars,
and the management and use of words is in
the hands of followers, who are now overtaking.
The blood trail on the ground comes from the blackberries
that have run wild at the edge of the forest this year.
I don't want to repeat again what we are,
those with understanding and those without,
couriers on active service with their faded words,
wanting to negotiate one last time: the humanly possible.
The mushroom yield is small this year,
first it was too dry, then too wet again,
now it's too cold, say the high lords of the weather;
instead, there are apples and pears and pumpkins in spades,
but above them there should be nothing but empty sky,
so the birds do not get in each other's way and the wasps
find their way home before it starts snowing tomorrow,
at the crack of dawn.

28

In order to escape Lethe and all its attractions,
I like to go to Schwabbrück, a small hamlet,
of maybe ten houses, clustered round an old farmstead.
Already at the first house I admire the wooden gauntree,
displaying its layers of wood so effortlessly and elegantly
as if destined for the museum, and the lawn round it too
looks as if it has been trimmed with nail scissors, no storm
stands a chance. If you want to make an omelette,
you have to break eggs, that's what comes to mind here.
Why on earth did God bequeath this twitching to chickens?
this adjustment of their whole body, this will
to ugliness. The hen is the best example of what
living constantly with humans leads to,
wrote Zbigniew Herbert, who loved chickens,
because they reminded him of poets, not only Polish ones.
Do chickens also prefer not to be eaten?
In front of the wood stands a man of wood smoking a pipe.
That smells good!, I call out to him, who can only hear
with his eyes. You won't get any further, he replies.
Above us, turtle clouds, grey-coloured junk.
Don't come too close, I call out to him, louder,
so as to make peace. In the windless chambers
of my heart dwells misfortune, these good tablets
make it transparent, you can see the bad blood,

flowing to the Lethe. Yes, to the motorway, he says meekly,
and stands there like a dowsing rod, unused for years,
though this is where the great treasures are stored.

29

A new terrace, a light-coloured one, so the slug knows
which way to turn when the heat increases.
I have no idea what family they belong to,
probably keeled slugs or tiger slugs,
there are hundreds of different species
that have shifted their shells into their soft body parts.
Why would one voluntarily give up one's house, why
not want to carry one's grave on one's back?
These creatures arrive on our terrace from one day
to the next. In a kind of mass tourism,
they crawl from northeast to southwest,
guided by the course of the stars and by the water.
No one wants them, likes to touch them, they leave
a nothingness behind when the slippery-slimy body
has squeezed into a gap between two tiles,
invisible to the naked eye. They are part of it,
even this snail-without-a-shell is our brother,
even if it can't find its feet on the ground.

My heart hopes for improvement, and the
stored pain of the shingles, the sore nerves
in the breaks in the skin, should disappear forever,
like the bark beetle, with which a conversation is pointless.
How long does impatience last? What it leaves behind,

the keelback slug, is a kind of autograph of its body,
right next to my shoe, as if that's supposed to mean something.

I have been reading too long among the arid sophistries
of a philologist, a miser of the imagination,
who wants to explain the world to me as tireless work
at the whole. But I am perfecting the art of Weltanschauung
and deep breathing, once more, and again,
and again and so on and forth.

30

Patience! It's still too early in the year, the world
still smells no different after rain. I had forgotten
that chestnut trees also grow on the streets of Turin,
la prima cosa bella, now I hear them bursting on the cobbles
and see the brown fellows bouncing over the gutter,
like in a Swedish poem. On my walk
through the villages, past the dark, brooding farmsteads,
I hear the sighing of the cows from the stables, the clanging
of pens and sometimes a distracted mooing,
which makes your heart go out. Don't chew so loudly,
dear beasts, I whisper to myself, inaudible to the great ears
of surveillance growing on the radio masts.
I can't help but think of the soundless dance of the rats,
    circa 1700,
a Flemish painting in the Städel. All this God allows to go on
when the day is long and a false understanding spreads
faster than approval, comfort and calm. I hear eight
little rat feet scratching as I reach the wood,
and tread carefully, as if I were walking on thin ice.
The wild rhubarb rustles under my feet . . .
Why has the lane emptied and the square,
why does everyone go back to their homes, preoccupied?
Because there are no more barbarians, simple as that
and just as unsolvable. Thin fronds of Himalayan balsam
catch hold of me, and the sounds of animals

that wander at night to find a hiding place
in the dark corridors of my brain, only to
leap into my dreams later on and dance like crazy.
Is it possible to build a wall with words? No.

31

for Angela von der Schulenburg

Sometimes I wonder how many times I've walked my
    crooked path,
under the beech trees, past the woodshed, and under the
    lime trees,
several times a day, with the blessing of the straight line,
into the mysterious twilight of the hundred thousand leaves
that know no beginning and no end, as if it were my goal
to get closer to infinity—in truth, of course,
to disperse the morphine in my body.
How many times have I listened to the buzzing of the bees,
the mighty choir that never changes its rhythm,
a requiem to death that does not want to die. The need
to change one's life dissolves over time, and the desire to
to read systematically in the book of nature is replaced
with amazement that everything has lasted so long, up to now.
A tern can fly sixty thousand kilometres, much further
than the range of the guns, and one day she will catch up with
death, who goes overland, along the back roads,
which are older than us, with travelling salesmen for company,
and dogs that in some countries are shot on sight.
On the left before me are the birches I rarely visit;
they are guarded by grass I don't want to trample, and
    further down

in the valley, especially 'when midday sleeps on space and time',
three more beeches shimmer in the air, that's where the birds
reside that want nothing to do with me, the better society.
I keep looking. I understand nothing, since I've been following
straight lines like a hen, and long for the zigzag
that confuses the gaze, the bitter neighbourhood,
where you don't care about being recognized.
I go back, past the woodshed again, to the house,
climb to the first floor and allow myself to fall gratefully
into the arms of the writing with a melancholy gesture.
My day begins.

32

On one of the longest days of the year
I dreamed of a talk show on TV,
the guests on which were turtles—all of them.
First the news, just as normal, at eight o'clock
with Jan Hofer and Marietta Slomka,
who kept interrupting each other, shoving
and snatching the mic out of each other's hands,
so that Susanne Daubner had to intervene,
then the weather with Plöger, who couldn't
get out a complete sentence for laughter,
and was waving at the weather map like a madman,
and finally, Anne Will in front of six turtles,
all with face masks and socially distanced,
talking about President Trump, as if he were
still alive. One of the turtles began
every sentence with: when I think of Lincoln,
but didn't get any further, Jan Hofer poured out water,
then tipped it over the heads of the turtles,
and a female turtle wanted a waste premium,
for old carrots. Particularly impressive was one
creature that needed a full hour to get ready.
It had come from the Prague Zoo, had known
the Kaiser and Kafka and had lived underground
for many years. Frau Will kept tapping her watch,

because time was running out, but the turtle was blind
and deaf and unstoppable. At four in the morning
I woke up, sleep was out of the question.

33

The many books I have read in the heartless time
now stand with their dog-eared pages and ugly markers
protruding from the edge like white flags begging for peace.
They have forgotten who the enemy is, so kill themselves
like the octopus gnawing at its own legs out of hunger,
which Pliny tells of. I once read a book about medieval pew
    rent in the Netherlands that gripped me more than
The Life History of the Hungarians, Budapest, 1941.
And then those glorious works on the Neoplatonic doctrine
    of the soul,
which you can't get enough of, especially if there is no
    other manual
advising how to learn to think without a fixed abode.
Some people consider the future, but I reflect on the forest
as the cradle of the human race, which does one good
    with Herder
and Harrison. The last, it is certain, will remain the last.
Since they are slower, they will find collisions, wars,
    catastrophes
easier to bear than the first who are always trying to get ahead
of progress and be the first to reach the end. So as not to lose
touch with life completely, I take a turn in the garden, then up
to the Bismarck tower and right, under the beech trees.
Two dogs approach me, then they stop and growl.
Dogs smell fear, my grandfather had drummed into me,

so I drive them away, shouting loudly, and return proudly
to the community of the fearful, loners and eccentrics,
who are loathe to negotiate with the strong. When the great crisis
becomes a permanent state, the third world war will have
broken out, without us noticing. The pigeons stagger about
like orthodox snobs in grey tailcoats, and two woodpeckers
cross the meadow like men of the world, as if tall grass were
a ludicrous whim of nature. I want to go back to my story
about a man who, with a melancholy gesture, gives up everything
he is and has, in order to be the most confident among all
the disappointed prophets. The sparrows seem like a barrel
of laughs.

34

We wanted to take a walk somewhere in the Pfaffenwinkel
but couldn't decide where exactly to go.
From here to Murnau, it's a stone's throw, as my
    grandmother,
who had learned to beware of exaggeration, liked to say,
speaking of Zeitz; it was two to Leipzig, but for us,
without a car or a horse and cart, everything was 'Back then',
and back then it was also only three stone's throws to Berlin.
Now, though, there was another reason to hesitate,
which was, at the same time, a reason to set off: it was
    drizzling (bad),
which meant there weren't many people about (good).
    When it looked
like rain, I used to say quite happily: It's about to pour,
so I could stay lying on the sofa (in Berlin), engrossed in *Cat
on a Hot Tin Roof*, which was playing at the theatre at
    that time.
The choice was *Cat* . . . in the Tribüne or *Don Carlos*,
with Rolf Henniger at the Schiller Theatre, not a difficult
    decision.
I loved my American childhood. It was drizzling slightly,
as we drove off the motorway at Murnau. You should
    turn back
if you can't see the trees any more, the local oracle says.
Richard had written that morning: when Germans begin

to hug trees, that's when it gets dangerous, he had it from
    Anders,
Günther Anders. I suddenly saw a white sheet fly
off a line and begin to float, a rain dance of sorts,
the mountains no longer visible, dreams of the Alps
erased with a wet paintbrush. And then the moor, the car park
empty, you could feel what nature does to people.
At school, when I raved about what I'd seen at the theatre,
I was told to come down from the trees. Here we were,
under them, pressed close to the scrawny birches, for the drizzle
had become hail, chunks lay like broken porcelain
on the stringy grass, white and green, the remains of
    the Meissen
service from which my grandmother had salvaged a single cup.
And I could already see the headline before me: two hikers,
with masks, discovered in the Murnauer Moos. Police are
    investigating.

35

More gibbet posts are springing up in and between the fields,
so that the birds of prey have an easier time finding their quarry.
Since we have been stood on two legs, it has also become
    easier for us
to see a long way. Not as far as the birds of the dead that even
use the sky, something we have long since abandoned. We use
drones to watch our neighbours wash their lettuce, this
our modest contribution to contemporary metaphysics.
Why hasn't the vulture become native in these parts?
Neither the buzzard nor the sparrowhawk has a mythical aura,
only the kite, which, however, considers it beneath its dignity
to use a perch just to finish off a mouse.
Bubbles rise from the larger puddles in the moor,
these days I don't find it hard to understand this language.
Last night, the right-wing thinkers were out on TV,
unimaginable philistines telling stories about their happy
    childhood,
and how they now wanted their children to . . . all of it
    cropped
to the usual format, no heretics, doubters, brooders,
    no apostates,
just this vile chaff begging for redemption with kitsch.
Bald heads in lederhosen, who in my homeland,
    Saxony-Anhalt

and Thuringia, seek to create fear and trembling with plastic
fairground guns, that normally shoot flowers.

I had forgotten to put a stone on top of my papers at home,
now they were scattered around the garden. How much infinity
can you generate in a lifetime? And with what operations?
I admired my trees, their acerbic reticence when cornered
between the trunk and the bark. After the end of quarantine,
I had in fact intended to go back to my roots, back home,
where the wrong side were trying to demolish my house.
Now I don't want to any more. I don't want to appear
in a photo with them, with this feigned naivety, under a gibbet,
on which a buzzard is waiting to kill a mouse.

36

In my notebooks, which I am now rereading,
to make them harmless for the prying eyes
of posterity—a stupid thought, because no one
will be interested in them anyway—I find sentences like this:
he dropped out of college and became a son-in-law.
A novel in micro-form, such as invented by Giorgio
 Manganelli.
Or a one-sentence story by Jürgen Becker. Maybe noted down
after a conversation? And, on the same page, but written
with a different device: he was unusually biased
and extraordinarily ill informed. Who is he? Is he still alive?
'Why should I be concerned about what I already know?'
 says Monsieur Teste.
He can talk. I know that the world is a wreck,
and can no longer be called whole. We know everything.
Or rather, we could know everything. In any case, we can't
say we didn't know. When I look up, I see the wind
in the grass, turning this way and that absentmindedly.
But the wind, too, follows a story that is worth knowing,
even if it cannot be described in a standard form.
The story of the wind, written by one who loves
trivial things but also the great theatre where words
lose their minds and leave us speechless.
The story of the wind, set to music for fingertips
and clenched fist, performed by a quintet of fools,

made up of those unlucky fellows in the open-air theatre
before my eyes, that knows nothing of art or pleasure,
whether it's for entertainment or just self-expression.
And then a lull in the wind, in which I hear
only the clicking of the app in my heart, in my room.
When I was a child, that's how the last notebook should begin
and end: a happy childhood without trembling or fear.

37

My room under the eaves has filled with paper,
with books, manuscripts by Syrian poets, newspapers
I have kept because they seek to enlighten me
about the state of the world, about trends in economics
after the pandemic, about thorny theological questions.
What is being contemplated in a contemplative time.
'Primates that lose contact with their group,
are not fetched back', I read in Sepp's book. Then what?
They die alone. Of course, you leave fingerprints,
sometimes they last longer on glossy films,
old tree trunks and in very humid conditions,
even on the window, if you stand there long enough.
How long do you go on allowing yourself to be enlightened?
When does it stop? Socrates was practising a song on the flute,
as his captors mixed the poison before his eyes.
He absolutely wanted to be able to play this song, he's supposed
to have said. I listen to the Sonata D 960 by Franz Schubert,
which I have heard many times, played by Dina Ugorskaja,
that Cornelius sent me. 'In this music, time / occasionally
    seems to stand still', says the pianist,
who came here, up the stairs with her piano,
to play me the Sonata and the *Moments Musicaux*,
and my heart stood still. For this moment,
which you can't measure, I knew everything about the world,
I had read all the books and taken in all the pictures,

and yet I was completely empty and ashamed of this emptiness.
To bring me back into the world, Dina Ugorskaja played
the three little piano pieces of D 946 until my eyes filled
with tears, sure proof that the pump was still working.

38

The morning looked as if it wanted to herald a brighter day,
it stood at the front door, went round the house and touched
   the windows.
I heard a cautious clink, a little cough, then the crow,
who lives in the back of beyond, and crows three times
as prescribed. Yesterday I went back to visit him,
on the path to Farchach that leads through the moor,
past the slowly sinking birch trees in their torn
uniforms. Reminiscent of preachers, pale, without conviction,
without passion. Behind the little water house live two goats,
with heavy beards and mighty horns, no one knows
how they found their way here. Maybe they followed
the water, from the Black Sea, along the Danube,
the Isar, the Würm and the Lüssbach, always upstream,
to here, where the crow lives and crows out of deepest conviction.
Jasmine, wood anemone, their scent almost suffocating.
Then the path narrows, only a child may pass, or
you must sing nursery rhymes, with all the verses, in any case
it's best to send your shadow on ahead, it knows
the way through the thorns. In Farchach the village fountain
is built into the foundations of the church. If you put your ear
to the stone, you hear all the liturgies the water has touched,
also the shofar and Gregorian chants, you can even
hear a lament from Cilicia if the blackbirds allow.
The water is so dark you can see yourself in it. But today

the morning is light, the lime trees are primed for the
    onslaught
of bees. You can breathe freely. Part of the air belongs to you.
The hand you use to touch the wood as it slowly warms
also belongs to you. The darkness you always carry with you,
but well hidden, so as not to create any half-light, in which
nothing can be seen any more. Yesterday on TV, a fearless
    camera
went through a meat factory; four thousand pigs are processed
per day. They hang on hooks on a rack, and each butcher
cuts off what he needs, the ears, the tiny tail,
the feet. All very clean and sad. A ballet for dead pigs.
No screams, no blood. The screams had already been sold,
the blood had seeped into the chalk-gravel layers of the planet.
But today is a beautiful day. I won't forget it.

39

for Axel Tangerding

The little theatre outside my window: a mouse with
    stage fright
flits across the hot tin roof of the shed, her first appearance
this summer; the satyr play of the blackbirds and the blather
of pigeons; in the background, two horses race across the
    meadow,
but no one knows if this has a deeper meaning.
Yesterday, even before the storm, I saw twelve cattle on
    the slope,
three of them were facing north, three facing west,
three south and three east, their hindquarters
all turned inwards. But the sea stood right at the top,
its rim was shaped like the rim of a cup,
like an open lily, and two thousand buckets of water
went inside. The piece was called 'The Bronze Sea'.
It opened as the sun was at its height and things lost
    their shadows,
in the bright midday light that fell vertically on the shed.
Before the shed, a washing line, clothes pegged out,
shirts and trousers that hung there until the sun went down
in the horizontal light, in the sweet sorrow of farewell.
When everything is dark, and it is very dark at night
in these parts, I am led by a few reeling fireflies
into the lawless time of sleep beyond the little theatre.

The bronze sea is drained, reflections dance
on the water, brief auspicious intervals for me,
then stagehands heave the heavy, dark banks
of cloud aside, ready for the entrance of the moon,
in another piece from the forbidden books:
'Death is not a Solution'. Every night the same piece, en suite,
with a change of cast now and then. If clouds rise
in the west, the old man with the stick says: there will be rain.
And it comes to pass. What matters is to endure it all,
day after day, night after night, as one glides over from the
no-longer of the formed into the not-yet of the unformed,
all summer long, until the leaves fall in my dreams,
in my theatre.

40

Today, caught between two huge thunderstorms
walking through the moor, a dog ran up beside me,
a strange creature, quite large, that could listen.
He didn't seem to have any particular preferences,
literature, music, philosophy, not even botany,
sundew, sedge, absolutely no interest,
not even our dear cotton grass could inspire him.
My father, for some unknown reason, loved music
by Tchaikovsky, which he sang on his long walks,
it haunted him like a sad necessity.
We walked past a pile of mouldy horse droppings
swarming with flies like a seething mass of notes.
The dog vanished to empty his bladder, then came back
to dawdle beside me, as if his real voice was silence.
Political issues? When I told him about populism,
the end of democracy, free elections,
he growled. We are more or less without rights,
he seemed to say: no one opens their mouth
when we are beaten. What is actually coming to an end,
he asked me, as we stopped by some blueberries,
everyone is worried about something coming to an end?
Sovereignty, I said dryly, sovereignty!
The essential decisions cannot be made
because every idiot wants to have a say. There were blueberries
en masse; naturally I had no bag with me again,

so I could wash them at home. A patchy shadow
flickered across the moor, and I hummed Tchaikovsky,
the Violin Concerto, a gospel of repetition,
and the preacher birds sang along at the top of their voices.
If you would like, I told the dog, we can arrange
to meet here at night, when the emptiness is filled
with fireflies, illusions and enchanting mirages.
But the dog had already gone on, dead ahead,
along the lunatic fringe and straight towards the end.

41

Summer surprised us, coming over the Starnberger See
with a shower of rain. It's time I remembered the toad,
which squeezed out from a crack in the foundations
of the house last night, puffing up its pocked toad-skin
like a blow-up mattress, in front, as a nozzle, its toothless mouth.
One of my grandmother's uncles, an expert on Job's tears,
lagrima de Job, saw his chance to do big business
by mixing juice from the glands of toads
with the dried false fruits of Job's tears
as an unbeatable remedy against any form of cancer.
(Against boils, he recommended dried millipedes,
a medicine appreciated only by initiates.)
In the year of my birth, he had visited my grandparents,
who, as Christians, wanted nothing to do with false fruits.
It was 1943, the year in which the collared dove was first
seen in Western Europe, a neophyte like the uncle,
who sold the false fruits of Job's tears as precious beads
for rosaries, albeit only in Catholic regions,
and not in Saxony-Anhalt, known for its toads
and its staunch Protestant faith.
In any case, the toad on our porch loved the rain shower,
it sat almost motionless, staring into space, as if it had to
decipher a parchment about a hitherto unexplored land,
in which lagrima de Job had put an end to cancer.

We were listening to Abbado playing the overture to
Haydn's 'Il mondo della luna' with the Chamber Orchestra
   of Europe,
the only institution in Europe that still believed in Europe,
and didn't know if we were hearing the beginning of the end,
or its end, which was a beginning. When Haydn's Overture
had finished, the toad had also disappeared, and with it
the rain, which went off to find another *waste land*
overnight.

42

Bellflowers grow everywhere, you can hear the sound
between Alaska and Sicily, and I used to hear it at Easter
on the Greek islands, under the Lindos Acropolis,
between the stones on the terrace of Grisha's house,
where, centuries before, Pindar had murmured one of his odes
(I think the eleventh), and in Pefkos, where Klaus and Erika
kept their hospitable lodgings. Bellflowers everywhere.
But I didn't know the bearded bellflower then,
that blooms in the meadow in front of the moor, where
it has no business being. A fugitive species that cuts a fine figure
alongside the many that are native here. *Campanila barbata*,
    hopefully
none of the purists will spot it while it's still so conspicuous.
Caliph Umar burned down the Library of Alexandria:
he thought a conscientious reading of the Koran enough,
and dreamed of an academy of supervised thinking
where the jinxed few and the small elite of scapegoats
could cram the scriptures. In the evening, the moor is deserted.
A haze begins to rise. It seems as if the world is lost
in infinity, despite the beauty and dignity
of the insignificant vista spread right before your eyes:
an abandoned snail shell, the iridescent skin of a snake.
If only these pigeons weren't here with their rambling
mediocrity, the authority of silence would come into its own.
Now it is good to have a song in mind, one that stays with you,

even if the text doesn't join in, just the pictures.
Should I pick the bearded bellflower? It all boils down
to this question. For thousands of years new plants
have become native here, there's no reason for that to stop,
so pick and go.

43

1.

Together with his son, Peter has mowed the lower meadow,
a ballet for two tractors just before the thunderstorm.
Now forty shiny bales stand on the earth,
as if they had been set up for a Dutch painting,
after nature. And two hours later, a rich green fringe
around a bright square, as if I were looking at the sky in *Seaport*
with the Embarkation of the Queen of Sheba by Claude Lorrain,
which I have just admired in an essay by Karlheinz Lüdeking.
And two hours later everything is totally red,
as if you were losing your mind looking at Dalí's skies.
Was paradise not round? In order to hold onto the truth,
you have to resist the real, writes Lüdeking.
And as I look up, Peter Huchel whispers in my ear,
it points / off into the grass / like a truth, and suddenly
the space is empty, as if a piece of laundry had lain there for ages.
There is still the real sky, but painted without talent,
with a washed-out brush, a gleaming dark watercolour,
more a case for the weather forecast than for the entreating eye.
The present form of this world is passing away, says the
    Apostle Paul.
I'll have to wait a long time for the blue-grey waves of grass
to grow back, the truth will not grow back.

2.

Now the white cat runs across the dark field
chasing the mice before it
into the hole.

44

The colour of the fruit of the rowan tree now
resembles the colour of the bricks in the shed;
they are spotted with moss, that is the colour
of rowanberry leaves. When, as now, there is a light wind,
the branches of the beech trees brush the roof of the shed,
as though they wanted to paint it, but with a wrong green.
Born under the voluptuous Ionian sky, I read yesterday
in a history of the history of art, and today it seems to me
that our sky is nothing but a miserable attempt to stand
in the way of a voluptuous sky. Anyway, why is the sky
masculine in German, and not feminine, or neuter at least.
Grammatical gender, says the Professor and delivers
her lecture on the applications that are of greatest value
in the human realm. Nothing more to be said.
In memoriam the snail: yesterday it was still crawling
single-mindedly across the bright tiles of the terrace, today
there is little left of it but a delicate veil.
I rest the flat of my hand on this last imprint of the silence
of a creature exposed to the noise of the world without
a voice of its own. Elsewhere, this creature is fried in hot fat
and eaten, jamais plus qu'un litre de vin.
Even the wind drops and for a moment interrupts
the scratching of beechnuts on the roof of the shed.
Why is the shed not gendered feminine? Here
humility reigns in the face of the kingdom of things, since

in this friendly asylum of brotherhood there is no hierarchy
among scythe and hoe and spade, though scythe
and hoe are feminine and only the spade masculine.
Summer afternoons, when dust columns turn in the
    slanting sun,
Leopardi comes by, Hölderlin's younger brother,
and both of them write a few lines in the soft dust,
very familiar, very puzzling and incomprehensibly clear:
all is vain, aside the beautiful illusion.

45

It's another of those days on which birds
shoot past my window, as if they're running late
and are afraid they will not be in time for the
transformation. Though every child knows . . . Only the robin
pauses for a few seconds. It sits on the
window frame looking at me, and shakes itself
like a religious zealot, shaking himself ready for prayer.
These days I find it easier to write down these beautiful
and sacred words and mix them with the mundane,
after spending an hour with the photographs of Stojan Kerbler,
with Janezek standing among the daisies,
and Sam in his heavy torn jacket, also with
Barantanje, the men in the cattle market with their crazy hats,
that look like black birds, flown past by chance,
so as not to miss a loud conversation about the price of milk.
I must cut back the ivy on the beech trees, soon it will be too late,
it has almost reached the crowns with its embrace.
Here it gets light and shifts into a realm where the blue haze
is inseparable from the whims and games of a day
in July. There is a photo of a young, smiling woman,
who stowed her piglets into a chest at the weekly market,
like the one we had at home to keep the food warm.
Dowries were once kept in chests like this, they say.
When you see images like this that never leave you,
you know that we cannot keep tally of the twentieth century.
The robin takes its leave. It bobs its tail and is gone,
as if it had never been, as if it had never seen me.

46

At last! Just in time all the bees have found a place
in one of the three lime trees, rehearsals can begin,
as soon as they have harmonized their humming. It's Palestrina
to start, pure monophony, fine-tuned
day by day to madrigals and lamentations,
and then for August the classics are on the programme,
to the bitter end. Listening to the Gregorian chants
of the bees makes you divide the world into days of salvation
and the rest. The birds hold their beaks, because they sense
what's right. When they start singing, we know
what's coming, and are happy: ah, the blackbird, predictable,
one to rely on. As for yourself, better keep your mouth shut,
but for other reasons, and head for home.
Best to pay heed to bears, because the bear not only
understands what the hunter says and thinks, it also
    understands us,
our conversations with ourselves about the thinning material
of life. And, of course, bears love honey.
No one expects us to say anything.
But then no one is expected at these concerts anyway.

47

for Gabriela Herpell

The terrace needs to be repaved,
because the old red tiles can no longer keep a lid
on the bubbling underworld beneath.
At first, grass sprang up in the gaps and could not be uprooted
without part of the whole coming loose right away,
then a kind of herbaceous gold lacquer stretched out its
    hairy arms
into the hot summer air. At first, I thought quite naively,
it might mean help for me, since back in the day wallflowers
were boiled down into a potion to be taken for the spleen.
But that was selfish thinking. This padded cushion
wanted nothing more than to cause turmoil above ground.
I used to be able to distinguish between wallflowers
and rockcresses, by glancing at the pods with their
lumpy seeds, but with age such knowledge
diminishes. So, the underworld was uncovered.

My God, what a bustle there was under the tiles!
Beetles, worms, slugs, larvae, and none of these creatures
ever wanted to return to the light. I had seen what I wanted
    to see,
there is a life beneath the stones that looks similar to ours.
No longer upright, because already on all fours, I crawled
about looking for a gap in the fence, I was in a panic.

The world did not seem very reliable to me, I wasn't even
sure if it still existed, the house, the trees and the hills,
the beautiful illusion that cannot separate itself from us.
Until I felt it, the wonderful nothingness at my back,
the thin voice behind me, which Montale knew something
    about.
Now it was time, I went into the house and held my right hand
out of the window, like Kevin, so the blackbird could
lay her eggs. The new tiles on the terrace are now white.

48

The question then is this: why can the seed
of the sunflower not produce a cactus?
Really, why not? I climbed up onto the raised hide
to view the world from above,
the paths through the moor that light up at dusk,
the rain falling on the blueberries that sit unconcerned,
and the nettles, the smell of which I love more than anything,
the rotten birch trees. I wanted to see the stream swell
and lose its iron-brown colour. But in fact
I just wanted to take a slightly higher point of view,
to reflect on Jürgen Goldstein's question.
On the way to the hide I found shards of porcelain,
remnants of a lost civilization buried in the bog,
sunk without trace. Others want to go to the moon,
to take a proper look at the earth,
the five wobbly rungs of the hide are enough for me.
It always felt weird and embarrassing to say human being,
or human beings, and if I ever allowed the word
humanity to pass my lips, I wanted to hide.
But up here, five metres above the ground and just a head
above the wet bushes, it is less difficult for me.
Below, a bird pecks obsessively in the boggy ground,
as if he sensed buried treasure. If you look further
what is unknown seems to multiply, that is the sad truth,
that makes some people happy, who can't get enough.

It doesn't have to be a cactus. But why not three hands
and four eyes so we can also see backwards, like flies,
without constantly turning round to see the enemy.
A large stage, without an audience and without other actors,
when the fog clears, I can see as far as the Alps.

49

This morning at four, the sun had just made its first attempts
to crest the rim of the horizon, I was woken
by a noise from the east side of the house. Nothing to see
at first glance. The blackbirds were busy
clearing away the aftermath of last night's thunderstorm,
the indifferent pigeons pretending not to know
that indifference is one of the worst mortal sins,
the bees had not yet decided how to spend the day,
and I was just about to go back to bed,
when I suddenly saw a group of Japanese-looking figures,
small, bald males with long, thin beards,
faces like last year's apples and scrawny fingers,
erecting a huge canvas behind the paddock with the horses,
then with the still-damp earth, painting a Japanese
landscape, in three or four stokes, a picture
of the flowing world that made me think of Hokusai.
If heaven had given me five more years, I thought,
pulled the blanket over my head and left the world to itself.
At seven, there was no sign of any of this. A group of bees
had fallen for the dwarf thyme, a purple rash
that had spread all over the meadow in front of the house.
You had to be careful not to get stung. The picture
of the flowing world had become a static one again,
a Bavarian idyll, without the great wave off Kanagawa
that I had been waiting for. You could still hear a noise

from the little men, a kind of fading burp and a distant giggle.
Only nothingness goes without saying, I said to the mirror,
that showed me, unmoved, like a clumsy copy of myself.

50

Enough now, I have
said almost everything or broached it.

Now things should
have the chance to say what they think.

Translator's Notes

The notes given here are not intended to be comprehensive; they simply fill in some of the references and background that might not be immediately familiar to non-German-speaking readers of the poems.

7

LINE 31. *But I go into the open, lie down on the meadow*: 'Komm! ins Offene, Freund' (Come! into the open, my friend) is the first line of the poem 'Der Gang aufs Land' (The Walk in the Country) by Friedrich Hölderlin (1770–1843). Although unfinished, the great elegy is well known for its musical setting and its invocation of longing, and especially that first line appears as the title of books and a biography of the poet.

8

LINE 15. *'The Word on Sunday'*: *Das Wort zum Sonntag* is a four-minute programme of religious content shown every Sunday on the main ARD TV channel.

9

LINE 11ff. *As a child, I was always meant to read*: The childhood reading consists of *Ein Kampf um Rom* (A Struggle for Rome), a novel by Felix Dahn 1876; Eugène Marais's *The Soul of the White Ant* (1925), a passionate study of the world of termites; and Eduard Stucken's *Die weißen Götter*, an epic account of, as its subtitle has it, 'the Spanish invasion of Mexico and conquest of the barbaric Aztec culture of the new World', which was

translated into English as *The Great White Gods* in the year of
its publication (1934).

14

LINE 16. *Him and his apple dolls*: The apple doll is a colloquial name
for what is best known in English at the Mandelbrot set.

16

LINE 7ff. '*Though distant is, at springtime, the lament*': The poem
returns to Friedrich Hölderlin, who after a mental breakdown,
lived out the last 36 years of his life in a tower in Tübingen. He
took to signing poems with the name Scardanelli, sometimes
adding a fictitious date. 'Though distant is, at springtime, the
lament' comes from the poem 'Der Frühling' (Spring); the next
quotation comes from 'Brod und Wein' (Bread and Wine) one
of his most famous elegies; 'For a long time, and in the distance,
thunder sounded' comes from the unfinished hymn, 'Wie wenn
am Feiertage . . .' (As when on holidays . . .); and the longer quo-
tation comes from Hölderlin's only novel *Hyperion; oder, der
Eremit in Griechenland* (Hyperion; or, the Hermit in Greece),
when the titular hero is dreaming of a perfect state of oblivious
unity in nature.

17

LINE 29. *Herr Diess* (*VW*): Herbert Diess was CEO of Volkswagen
(2018–22), who in 2021 demanded a fourfold increase in CO_2
tax to offset the extra expense of making electric cars and also
presided over the diesel emissions scandal.

LINE 31. *No beautiful country in this time*: 'Kein schöner Land in
dieser Zeit' (No Country More Beautiful in This Time) is one
of the most popular German folksongs. It has been set to music
and the oft-referenced title is varied in this poem. The last lines
quote one of the verses.

19

LINE 10. *'its pale heads heavy as metal'*: Ted Hughes' poem 'Snowdrop' contains this line.

LINE 26. *But if the salt has lost its flavour* ...: Matthew 5:13

LINE 33–34. *'The message of the yew tree is blackness ...'*: From Sylvia Plath's poem 'The Moon and the Yew Tree'.

20

LINE 29. *From the pointed mouth of the burgher*: In this line, the poem plays on the burgher's pointed hat in the first line of Expressionist poet Jakob von Hoddis' fragmentary vision of apocalypse 'Weltende' (End of the World, 1911).

23

LINE 8. *Your refrain was not in vain*: August Heinrich Hoffmann von Fallersleben (1798–1874) was a progressive German poet, probably most famous for his 'Song of the Germans' that begins 'Deutschland Deutschland über alles', which was set to music by Hadyn in 1871. His children's songs are also very well known: including 'Frühlingsbotschaft' (Spring Tidings), set by Richard Strauss, in which the call of the cuckoo successfully drives winter from the fields ('your refrain was not in vain' for 'was du gesungen, ist dir gelungen'). Another of his poems 'Der Kuckuck und der Esel' (The Cuckoo and the Donkey) tells of the competition between a cuckoo and a donkey to sing.

LINE 27. *Lynghi*: One of the several names that friends called the post-war German poet Peter Rühmkorf (1929–2008).

LINE 31. *Des Knaben Wunderhorn*: Literally, 'The Boy's Magic Horn', this is a collection of German folk poems and songs edited by Achim von Arnim and Clemens Brentano, and published in three volumes between 1805 and 1808.

24

LINE 27. *'Karst' poet*: Scipio Slataper was a Trieste poets born in 1888 who died in the First World War in 1915. He is famous for his essay 'Il mio carso' (My Karst) a lyrical essay celebrating the local landscape.

LINE 28. *love-lies-bleeding*: 'Stiefmütterchen', literally little step-mother, is a common name for the pansy in German. There are many alternative names in English too: love-lies-bleeding, love-in-idleness, Johnny-jump-up; godfathers and grandmothers, heartsease, etc., though probably not as well known.

24

LINE 13. Ferdinand van Kessel, *The Dance of the Rats* (*c.* 1690), Städel museum, Frankfurt am Main.

31

LINE 21. The quotation comes from Friedrich Nietzsche's poem 'Nach neuen Meeren' (Towards New Seas).

36

LINE 6. *Georgio Mangenelli*: His 1979 work *Centuria: cento piccoli romanzi fiume*, where each of the hundred stories are one page long.

LINE 7. *Jürgen Becker*: The German writer's 2009 novel *Im Radio das Meer* (*The Sea in the Radio: Journal Sentences*) consists of a sequence of single sentences.

LINE 11. *Monsieur Teste:* In Paul Valery's *Monsieur Teste* (1896), the French modernist imagines a man bent on living a fully conscious life.

39

LINE 26. *Death is not a solution*: Says Fritz Lang, playing himself, in Jean-Luc Godard's film *Le Mépris* (Contempt, 1963).

41

LINES 1–2. The opening lines refer to T. S. Eliot's *Waste Land* (1922).

43

LINE 14. The quotation from Peter Huchel comes from the poem 'Alkaios' (Alkaois), here taken from the volume *These Numbered Days* (Martyn Crucefix trans.) (Bristol: Shearsman Books, 2019).

44

LINE 26. *in this friendly asylum*: In Hölderlin's 1799 poem 'Mein Eigentum' (My Property), poetry is the garden addressed as 'mein freundliches Asyl' (my friendly asylum).

LINE 33. *all is vain*: Giacomo Leopardi's *Canzoni* (1820–23): 'All is vain aside beautiful illusions and delectable frivolities' (l. 3990).

47

LINE 23. *The world did not seem very reliable to me*: In the existential anxiety, one probably hears an echo of Rilke's first 'Duino Elegy' (1923): 'daβ wir sind nicht sehr verläβlich zu Haus sind / in der gedeuteten Welt' (that we are not very reliably at home in the interpreted world).

LINE 29. *out of the window, like Kevin*: Seamus Heaney's 'St Kevin and the Blackbird' (1996).

The poet Michel Krüger had begun therapy for leukaemia just as the Covid-19 pandemic broke out. He wrote these poems under quarantine in his house near the Starnberger See. During that time, he and his wife were not permitted to leave the garden or receive visitors aside from the postman and the doctor—a rule, he explains, they gratefully circumvented, if only occasionally. Twenty of the cycle of poems were sent to the *Süddeutsche Zeitung*, which published them weekly in 2020 to great acclaim.

Thanks to Michael Krüger for patiently answering queries and Iain Galbraith for companiable sleuthing. I was fortunate to be able to begin work on this project just across the lake from the wooden house in question, during a residency in the Künstlerhaus Villa Waldberta and the Lyrik Kabinett Munich, supported by the Munich Artist in Residence scheme.

Karen Leeder